You
know *you're*
Filipino
if...

You know you're Filipino if...

A Pinoy Primer

Selected and edited by
Neni Sta. Romana-Cruz

Drawings by
Dindo Llana

Tahanan Books

Manila

Published by Tahanan Books
A division of Tahanan Pacific, Inc.
P.O. Box 9079, MCS Mailing Center
1299 Makati City, Philippines

Designed by Roberto T. Canlas
Printed in the Philippines by Island Graphics
10 9 8 7 6

National Library of the Philippines
Cataloging-in-Publication Data

Recommended entry:

Cruz, Neni S.R.
    You know you're Filipino
if... : a pinoy primer / selected
and edited by Neni Sta. Romana-Cruz
; drawings by Dindo Llana. -
Makati City : Tahanan Books
c1997
    1 v

    1. Philippine - Manners and customs.
I. Llana, Dindo.   II. Title.

GT3405P5   1997   390.009599   P973000010
ISBN   971-630-080-8 (pbk.)
ISBN   971-630-081-6 (pbd.)

For Elfren, Tanya, Roel, Aina, Norman,
Victor, and Christopher

—N.S.R.C.

For Joanne and my family

—D.L.

Contents

Introduction

This collection first appeared on an electronic grapevine called the Internet. It began as a tongue-in-cheek list of quirks and traits that made Filipinos stand out in a crowd. "You Know You're Filipino If..." became so popular with *Pinoys* here and abroad that it produced several spinoffs, including the rib-tickling "You May Be Married to a Filipina If...."

This is the first time that I've used the Internet as the main source of material for a book. Dubbed the "rummage sale in the sky" and the "library of libraries," the information available on the Web is both a blessing and a curse. Now, literally at our fingertips, the Internet provides unlimited access to the information we seek and everything else besides.

Given this global communication tool, the mass circulation of the "You Know You're Filipino If…" lists was inevitable. Because these lists were catchy and witty and struck a familiar chord, they were eagerly passed on to friends and relations in the true fashion of the Pinoy extended family. New entries were added and these lists quickly became everybody's property. It is for this reason that their authorship cannot be attributed to any one person. It struck me how this compendium has assumed the characteristics of folklore. For, like folklore, it has no author, and it belongs to everyone.

In researching this book, I enjoyed many a laugh over our amusing, often inimitable, mannerisms. But I also became aware that some attributes were derogatory. I did not feel comfortable perpetuating these putdowns, until I saw here an opportunity to showcase positive Filipino traits as well. A concerned friend who deeply loves our country wondered if I could deliver a book with enough complimentary attributes. Well, I discovered that it *is* possible!

In the course of my research I was surprised to discover that we Filipinos make poor interview subjects for a book of this sort. Many of us are so comfortable with the way we are that we are largely unaware that what we think and do is unique. My expatriate friends provided the most interesting insights because our cultural quirks and idiosyncracies are magnified a thousandfold in their company.

When I was in school, there was a great deal of debate about the true identity of the Filipino. *What does it mean to be Filipino?* Survivors of a medley of colonial influences, many Filipinos were uncertain of who and what we were. We confused ourselves and others. It seemed futile to even talk about nationhood and nationalism when we had been so hopelessly "Coca-Colanized."

Perhaps it is in the company of non-Filipinos where Filipinos truly stand out. The last few decades have witnessed a great migration of Filipinos in search of a better life. Even in strange lands and far from home, the indefatigable Pinoy spirit often prevails, thanks in great part to an optimistic outlook that is deeply ingrained in our culture.

This book pays tribute to all that is Filipino. If you should catch a glimpse of yourself in these pages, then this book has done its job. And if you find yourself laughing, so much the better. So kick off your *tsinelas*, sit back, and enjoy this lighthearted romp!

Neni Sta. Romana-Cruz

How to Use This Book

Just how Pinoy are you?

This book will help you find out just that!

We've come up with 11 categories detailing the unmistakable characteristics that make Pinoys stand out in a crowd.

Beside each item you will find an empty box. Tick the box if the entry applies to you.

Once you've reached the end of the book, tally the number of boxes you've ticked to see how you scored. Then refer to the chart on pages 83–85 at the back of the book.

So, test yourself. *Gaano ka ka-Pinoy?*

You
know you're
Filipino
if...

Family Matters

☐   You're related to everyone.

☐   Your middle name is your mother's maiden name.

☐   Your parents call each other "Mommy" and "Daddy."

☐   You have uncles and aunts named Boy, Girlie, or Baby.

☐ · You have relatives with the letter "h" slipped into their names, as in Jhun, Mhike, Bhen, and Sahmmeeh.

☐   You have relatives whose nicknames consist of repeated syllables, such as Jun-Jun, Ling-Ling, and Mon-Mon.

☐   You call the parents of your friends and your own parents' friends *"Tito"* and *"Tita."*

☐ All your children have four or five names.

☐ You greet your elders by touching their hands to your forehead.

☐ You always kiss your relatives on the cheek whenever you enter or leave the room.

☐ Your grandmother greets you by smelling your cheek.

☐ The prospect of sending your elderly parents to a nursing home is inconceivable.

☐ You abide by your parents' house rules even if you are over 18.

☐ You live with your parents until—and at times even after—you're married.

☐ You think nothing about hosting a houseful of *balikbayan* relatives for weeks on end—and can still smile about it.

☐ You demand that your children sing and dance to amuse your friends and relatives.

☐ You'll sell, borrow, beg, or steal the last carabao to send your children and siblings to university.

Where We Live

☐ Your house has a distinctive aroma.

☐ You can't build or buy a house without first consulting a *feng shui* expert.

☐ You can't build a house unless you first bury religious medals and money at the site.

☐ You decorate your living room wall with your family's framed diplomas and certificates and plaques.

☐ On your living room wall you display a shield bearing "The Weapons of Moroland" alongside a giant wooden rosary and wooden *tinikling* dancers or Ifugao heads.

☐ You decorate your dining room wall with a giant wooden spoon and fork and a picture of the Last Supper.

☐ You keep your furniture wrapped in plastic.

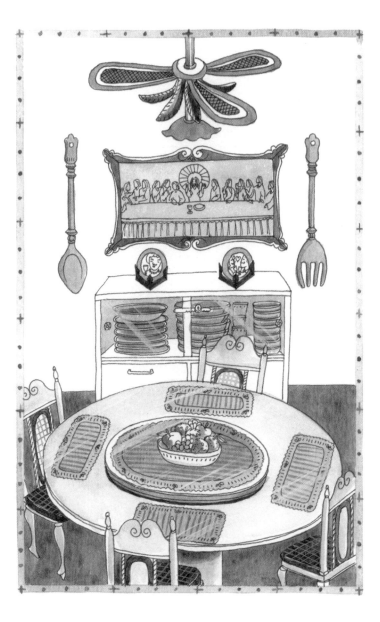

☐ You keep a Sto. Niño shrine in your living room.

☐ You keep a statue of a big, fat, laughing Buddha—with those pesky little kids crawling all over him—for good luck.

☐ Most of your home decor is made of wicker.

☐ Your house has a "dirty" kitchen and a "clean" kitchen.

☐ You keep a fly swatter in your kitchen.

☐ You cook with clay pots and firewood on a stone stove.

☐ Your kitchen table has a vinyl tablecloth.

☐ You recycle plastic shopping bags as garbage bags.

☐   You own a "Footsteps in the Sand" poster.

☐   You use the finest things you own only when there's company.

☐   You have a piano no one plays.

☐   You use a bolo to cut the grass in the yard.

☐   You keep a *tabo* in your bathroom.

☐   You use a halved coconut husk to polish the floor.

☐   You own a "barrel man."

Health and Hygiene

☐ You shower at least once a day.

☐ You use a stone to scrub yourself in the shower.

☐ You shampoo with dried tree bark.

☐ You prefer hand-washed to machine-washed laundry.

☐ You prescribe a ginger brew and a salt mouthwash to treat sore throats.

☐ You insist on having an extra bed in your hospital room.

☐ You place equal importance on Western medicine, traditional medicine, homeopathic remedies, wholistic cures, and healing by a member of the clergy and by a lay person.

Herbal Medication for Abscesses and Boils:
Gumamela leaves and flowers poultice: Chop 5 leaves and 2 flowers. Apply directly on abscess or boil as poultice, 2 times a day.
Langka juice or sap compress: Mix juice or sap with a little vinegar. Warm mixture and use it for hot compress. Use small pieces of clean cloth or gauze as compress. Apply for 20 minutes, 2 times a day.

☐ You use Vicks Vapor Rub as an insect repellant.

☐ You have ageless skin, thanks to the high humidity of the tropics.

☐ Your skin is a perpetual tan that makes it resistant to skin cancer.

Salabat

Boil 3 tBsp chopped giNger IN 3 cups of water. StraiN.

The Way We Eat

☐ You eat with your hands.

☐ You eat more than three times a day.

☐ You think a meal is not a meal without rice.

☐ You use your fingers to measure the water you need to cook rice.

☐ You can't eat a meal without using a large spoon with your fork.

☐ You don't need a knife to cut your food.

☐ You think sandwiches are snacks, not meals.

☐ You feel compelled to greet anyone who sees you eating with the words "Let's eat."

☐ You swing your legs when you like the food.

These are Filipino BBQ. These are grilled and sold in the streets. These are dipped in vinegar before these are eaten. Match these drawings with their names.

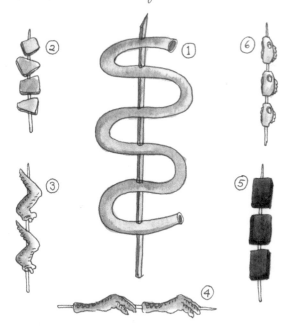

(A) __Adidas__
chicken feet

(B) __PAL__
chicken wings

(C) __IUD__
chicken intestines

(D) __Helmet__
chicken heads

(E) __Betamax__
chicken blood

(F) __Walkman__
Pigs' Ears

☐ You feed all your visitors.

☐ You always cook too much.

☐ You never take the last morsel of food on the table, but offer it to your guests instead.

☐ You always leave room at the dining table for a couple of unexpected or uninvited guests.

☐ Your dining table has a merry-go-round (lazy susan) in the middle.

☐ You bring *baon* to work everyday.

☐ You keep your stove covered in aluminum foil when not in use.

☐ You recycle bottles into water containers and store these in the fridge.

☐   You wash and reuse disposable styrofoam cups, plastic spoons and forks, and aluminum wrappers. You also love recycling paper plates by covering them with wax paper.

☐   Your pantry is never without Spam, Vienna sausage, corned beef, and sardines.

☐   You love to eat what others mistakenly refer to as "rotting fish."

☐ You prop up your knee while eating.

☐ You always leave a morsel of food on your plate at a party lest you appear famished.

☐ You throw a party, and everyone is fighting to chop the leathery skin off a dead pig.

☐ You're excited by the prospect of sucking the fat off pigs' knuckles.

Adobo:
Cut meat into cubes
Mix with vinegar
soy sauce and gar-
lic. Simmer until
dry. Fry Adobo
for Breakfast.

Circles on table cloth

☐ You can't enjoy a meal without *patis, toyo,* vinegar, banana catsup, or *bagoong.*

☐ Your tablecloths are stained with toyo circles.

☐ You love sticky desserts and salty snacks.

☐ You eat fried chicken with catsup and unripe fruits with giant salt crystals.

☐   You eat fried Spam and hot dogs with rice.

☐   You eat mangoes with rice—with great gusto.

☐   You enjoy chocolate rice pudding and dried salted fish for breakfast.

☐   Your idea of a classy, expensive champagne is Asti Spumante.

☐   You prefer *bistek* to beef steak.

☐   You like sweet spaghetti.

☐   You love "dirty" ice cream.

☐   You eat purple yam ice cream.

☐   When dining out, you always fight over who will pay for dinner.

☐   You instinctively grab a toothpick after every meal.

☐   You love to eat, yet often manage to stay slim.

The Way We Drive

☐   You hang your left arm out the window and wave your hand to signal a left turn.

☐   You hang a rosary on your car's rear view mirror.

☐   You drive a jeep with your family name prominently written on the rear.

☐   You tail an ambulance just to beat the traffic.

☐   Your car chirps like a bird, plays a tune, or simply attracts attention when you put it in reverse.

☐   Your car horn can make at least three different sounds.

☐   You can squeeze 15 passengers into your five-seater car without a second thought.

Wang-wang, alarm, and powerlocks from Banaue

Ski rack from Cavite

Luminous Rosary and image of the Virgin Mary from Baclaran

Für Elise by Beethoven (when in reverse)

Seat cover from National Bookstore

Plate No. Neon from Greenhills

Yellow fog light from Cubao

Dashboard carpeting from Rue de La Div

Mag wheels and tailpipe from Timog

☐   You keep your car seats covered in plastic.

☐   You think traffic regulations are recommendations, not rules.

☐   Signs like "No left turn" or "No U-turn" apply to everybody but yourself.

☐   You think a yellow light means "Step on the gas, you'll make it!" and the guy behind you is counting on you to do just that.

☐   You drive where there's space, even if it means converting a two-lane street into a four-lane road.

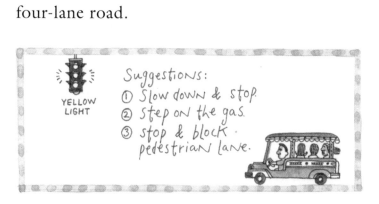

YELLOW LIGHT

Suggestions:
① Slow down & stop.
② Step on the gas.
③ stop & block pedestrian lane.

☐ You know the rules of the road: In the event of an impasse, the driver to first achieve eye contact with the other driver has lost his nerve and must give in.

☐ You know that no last minute maneuver on the road is considered presumptuous.

☐ Your ability to create your own parking space in a totally jampacked parking lot puts Houdini to shame.

The Way We Pray

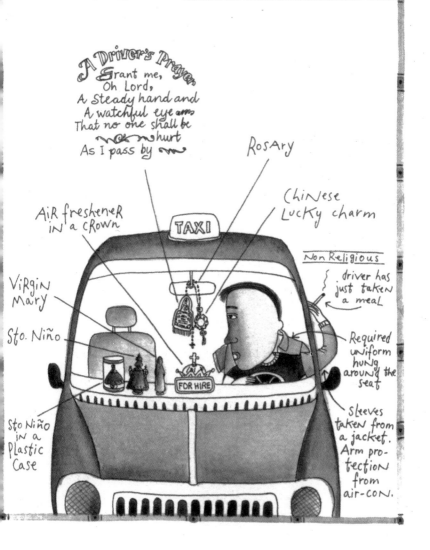

A Driver's Prayer
Grant me,
Oh Lord,
A steady hand and
A watchful eye
That no one shall be
hurt
As I pass by

Rosary

Chinese
Lucky charm

Air freshener
in a crown

TAXI

Non Religious
{ driver has
just taken
a meal

Virgin
Mary

Sto. Niño

FOR HIRE

Required
uniform
hung
around the
seat

Sleeves
taken from
a jacket.
Arm pro-
tection
from
air-con.

Sto Niño
in a
Plastic
Case

☐   Your idea of Lenten penitence is corporal punishment.

☐   You spend Holy Week either performing acts of penitence or vacationing.

☐   You get together with family at a cemetery on All Saints' Day to eat, drink, and tell stories by your loved ones' graves.

☐   You can crack jokes, play cards or mahjong, and drink beer at funeral wakes and not feel irreverent.

☐   You feel compelled to keep 24-hour vigils at funeral wakes.

☐   You think the Christmas season begins in September and ends in January.

☐   Christmas isn't Christmas without a *parol* and a *belen*.

Motorist's Guide to Passing a Church in the Philippines: ① Hold the Rosary or any religious image, preferably the Sto. Niño or Virgin Mary, hanging in your Rear view mirror. ② Mumble a prayer ③ Make the sign of the cross.

Meditation in the streets of Manila: You need to Bring a rosary, preferably the ring kind. Pray the rosary until you get to your destination. Another way is to read those booklets of Novenas.

☐   There are at least **50** people on your Christmas gift list.

☐   You unwrap Christmas presents ever so carefully, so you can reuse the wrappers and bows for next year.

☐   You can't make an important decision without praying a novena.

☐   You touch your chin with your thumb every time you make the sign of the cross.

☐   You make the sign of the cross every time you pass a church.

☐   You make three wishes every time you visit a church for the first time.

☐   You are as passionate about love as you are about religion.

The Way We Travel

☐ Your second piece of luggage is a balikbayan box.

☐ You don't know the meaning of traveling light.

☐ You've mastered the art of packing a suitcase to double capacity.

☐ Packing entails jumping up and down on your suitcase to get it to close.

☐ You're often seen at airports standing next to eight boxes.

☐ Your carry-on luggage requires a small forklift.

☐ You insist that customs officers who open your luggage repack everything "just the way it was."

☐ You unpack and repack luggage and boxes in public in international airports.

☐ You collect items from airlines, hotels, and restaurants as "souvenirs."

☐ You feel compelled to give *pasalubong* to all your friends and relatives each time you return from a trip.

☐ You drive a car which proudly bears foreign license plates to publicize your latest travel destination.

The Way We Shop

☐ You can't make a purchase without haggling.

☐ You can't resist buying items on sale—even if you don't need them.

☐ Everything in your house was bought on sale.

☐ It's an absolute must to go duty-free shopping even when you've come home with several balikbayan boxes.

☐ After buying a new pair of shoes, you keep the box for storing an old pair of shoes.

☐ You check the labels on clothes to see where they were made.

☐ You use paper foot outlines when buying shoes for friends and relatives.

Buying Shoes in Absentia

① Cut Along outline of Foot | ② Fold lengthwise then insert in shoe | ③ Flatten inside shoe

☐ You're a fashion victim.

☐ You always know someone who can get you a good deal on jewelry or electronics.

☐ You lamented the withdrawal of the US bases if only because it meant the end of PX shopping.

Pinoy Body Language

☐ You point with your lips.

☐ You can convey **30** messages with your facial expressions.

☐ You greet one another by raising your eyebrows or tossing your head.

☐ You hold your palms together in front of you and say "Excuse, excuse" when you pass in between people or in front of the TV.

PINOY BODY LANGUAGE DANCE

① March in place as you raise your eye brows repeatedly and wave your hands

② Turn right and nod with palm folding up

③ TURN to the other side with arm raised & finger pointed then point your lips.

④ Turn to other side, & scratch head

⑤ Put palms together infront of you, stoop, & shuffle in between people as you say "excuse, excuse."

☐ You scratch your head when you don't know the answer.

☐ You smile all the time for no reason at all.

☐ You ask for the bill at a restaurant by making a rectangle in the air.

☐ You cover your mouth when you laugh.

The Way We Speak

□   You respond to a *"Hoy!"* or a *"Pssst!"* in a crowd.

□   You'll answer *"Malapit lang!"*—no matter the distance—when asked how far away a place is located.

□   You can use ambiguous words like *"kwan"* and *"ano"* and yet be perfectly understood by other Filipinos.

□   You refer to your Mercedes Benz as the *"chedeng."*

□   Goldilocks is more than a fairy tale character to you.

□   Your sneeze sounds like *"A-ching"* instead of *"Ahh-choo."*

□   You refer to anything old as "pre-war."

☐   You love to use the following acronyms:
- CR for comfort room
- DI for dance instructor
- DOM for dirty old man
- TNT for *tago nang tago*
- KJ for killjoy
- KSP for *kulang sa pansin*
- OA for over-acting
- MU for mutual understanding
- TL for true love
- BF for boyfriend
- GF for girlfriend

☐   You refer to a person whose name escapes you as *"Si ano."*

☐   You greet people you haven't seen in a long time by saying, "Long time, no see!"

☐   You say *"Uy!"* or *"Aray!"* instead of "Oops!"

☐ Instead of "I beg your pardon?" you say *"Ha?"*

☐ You say "For a while" instead of "One moment, please" or "Please hold."

☐ You say "hand-carry" instead of "carry-on luggage."

☐ You say "shades" instead of "sun glasses" and also use them as hairbands.

☐ You refer to power interruptions as "brownouts."

☐ You call foreign-made commodities "PX" goods.

☐ You say "comfort room" instead of "toilet."

☐ You "open" or "close" the lights.

☐ You call the waiter "boss" or *"brod."*

☐ You say "for take-out" instead of "to go."

☐ You ask for "Colgate" instead of "toothpaste."

☐ You ask for "Kleenex" instead of "tissue paper."

☐ You say "Cutex" instead of "nail polish."

☐ You say "Mongol" instead of "pencil."

☐ You refer to the refrigerator as the "ref" or the "pridyider."

☐ You say "canteen" instead of "cafeteria."

☐ You say "rubber shoes" instead of "sneakers."

☐ You say "ballpen" instead of "ball point pen."

☐ You're perfectly understood by fellow Filipinos, although you seldom mean what you say and say what you mean.

The Way We Are

☐ You're always late.

☐ You'd rather be caught dead than arrive at a party on time.

☐ You can't throw anything away.

☐ You say "Maybe" or "I'll try" when actually you mean "No."

☐ You have a ready answer for every question, no matter how ludicrous, because you don't want to say "I don't know."

☐ You beat around the bush, use euphemisms, and resort to third parties when conveying unpleasant news.

☐ You cope with a serious situation by turning it into a humorous one.

☐ You'll go into debt for a celebration.

☐ You can sing and dance at the drop of a hat.

☐ You have a high threshold for pain and suffering.

☐ You take to the streets during a coup d'etat to satisfy your curiosity and buy ice cream, peanuts, cotton candy, and cigarettes from vendors while ducking machine-gun fire.

☐ You have a high tolerance for corruption and a short, forgiving memory when it comes to history.

☐ You like everything imported.

☐ There are always two or three pairs of slippers deposited at your doorstep.

☐   You always prefer to sit in the shade than bask in the sun.

☐   You use an umbrella in fair and foul weather.

☐   You *never* discuss the weather.

☐   You spend 3/4 of your spare time playing or watching basketball.

☐   You believe in chivalry. You still hold doors open for, give up your seat to, and carry the bags of women and the elderly and assist them when boarding or alighting from vehicles.

☐   It makes you uncomfortable to be praised or flattered.

☐   You ask people you have just met how many children they have and what their spouses do for a living.

☐   You love ballroom dancing and karaoke.

☐   You always ring a doorbell twice, assuming that the first ring was not heard.

☐   You let the phone ring twice before answering, lest you appear overly eager.

☐ You hang your clothes out to dry.

☐ You don't know the meaning of angst.

☐ You love to laugh at yourself and at others.

What We Mean

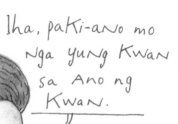

Glossary

ano	whatchamacallit
"Aray"	"Ouch"
bagoong	shrimp paste
balikbayan	a Filipino returning to the Philippines
baon	a packed meal
belen	crèche
bistek	thin slices of seasoned beef
brod	short for brother
feng shui	Chinese astrology
"Gaano ka ka-Pinoy"	"How Pinoy are you"
"Ha"	"What"
"Hoy"	"Hey, you"
Ifugao	an indigenous northern Philippine people
kulang sa pansin	a person who craves attention
kwan	whatchamacallit
"Malapit lang"	"It's very near"
"Malayo ka pa"	"You have a long way to go"
parol	Christmas lantern
pasalubong	coming-home present
patis	fish sauce
Pinoy	Filipino
Pinoy na Pinoy	truly Filipino
"Pssst"	"Hey, you"

"Si ano"	"What's his name"
Sto. Niño	Christ Child
tabo	dipper
tago nang tago	an illegal alien
tinikling	a Filipino folk dance with bamboo poles
tita	aunt
tito	uncle
toyo	soy sauce
tsinelas	slippers
"Uy"	"Oops"
"Wala nang hihigit pa sa 'yo"	"You are second to none"

How You Scored

PeNoy Ka `day!

0-35 pts. You scored a big, fat egg. You must be a foreigner. Take some time to brush up on your Pinoyness.

PiNoy was Here!

36-70 pts. Leaving a toyo stain on the tablecloth does not a Pinoy make. You've got to leave a stronger mark than that!

Far pa the Pinoy.

71-100 pts. *Malayo ka pa!* You've got a ways to go before you are considered truly, madly, and deeply Pinoy!

Amoy Na amoy Ka, Pinoy!

101-135 pts. You look like a Pinoy. You walk like a Pinoy. You talk like a Pinoy. You even smell like a Pinoy. You must be Pinoy!

Pang-display!

136-170 pts.   Congratulations! You're a bonafide Pinoy, truly deserving of this trophy.

Pinoy, hang this. Quick!

171 and up.   *Pinoy na Pinoy.* 100 proof. You are Pinoy through and through. *Wala nang hihigit pa sa 'yo!*

Acknowledgments

My grateful thanks to Virgilio Almario, Vincent Benedicto, Rosal Bulaong, Leo Carpio, Punch Casal, BeAnn Castro, Caroline Castro, Eduardo Delgado, Leah S.R. Dumlao, Martin Hall, Pat Jardiniano, Yvette Jarencio, Dindo Llana, Ging Manansala, Agnes Manlangit, Mariles Ebro Matias, Therese Ng, Cecilia Parrenas, Mina Ramirez, Jose Raymundo, Rowena Rodriguez, Randy Rosales, Letty Sala, Tony Samson, Chiara Savino, Raissa Segovia, Nena Sia, Val Solisa, Dali Soriano, Lory Tan, Arne Tangherlini, Gerardo Ubaldo, Kim and Randy Williams, Cheryl Wells, Red Yerro, and to the many anonymous Internet sources.

—Neni Sta. Romana Cruz

About the Author

Neni Sta. Romana-Cruz won the 1993 National Book Award for Children's Literature for her book *Why the Piña Has a Hundred Eyes and Other Classic Philippine Folk Tales About Fruits*, published by Tahanan Books for Young Readers. Her biography of Gabriela Silang, written for Tahanan's Great Lives series, received a 1992 National Book Award citation for excellence. She has also written a collection of essays titled *Sundays of Our Lives*. Her latest book is the best selling *Don't Take a Bath on a Friday: Philippine Superstitions and Folk Beliefs*, also published by Tahanan Books.

After graduating *cum laude* from St. Scholastica's College, Ms. Cruz pursued a master's degree in English literature at the Ateneo de Manila University.

Ms. Cruz has chaired the Philippine Board on Books for Young People and is a children's book critic and freelance journalist. She currently heads the Children's Media Center at the International School, Manila, and teaches a writing course for talented elementary school students.

The author lives with her husband, Elfren, and their children Tanya, Roel, and Aina in Parañaque, Metro Manila.

About the Artist

Dindo Llana received his bachelor's degree in fine arts from the University of the Philippines. In 1995 he received the bronze medal in the Art Association of the Philippines Art Competition. He is the illustrator of *The Secret Is in the Sauce; Ayokong Pumasok sa Paaralan; Hugis Bugis Wugis*; and *Anna Learns to Swim*, which in 1996 was a finalist for the National Book Award for Best Children's Literature. He is a member of Ang Ilustrador ng Kabataan (INK), an organization of young artists devoted to children's book illustration.

Mr. Llana is currently an art director at an advertising agency. He lives in Quezon City.